Merry Christmas From Georgia

by

Michelle Stone

Michelle Stone

McClanahan
Publishing House

International Standard Book Number 0-913383 71 6
Library of Congress Catalog Card Number 00-104154

Cover design and book layout by James Asher Graphics

Manufactured in the United States of America

All book order correspondence should be addressed to:

McClanahan Publishing House, Inc.
P.O. Box 100
Kuttawa, KY 42055
270-388-9388
1-800-544-6959
email: kybooks@apex.net
www.kybooks.com

It is with love that I dedicate this book to my two children, who have brought me much joy!

Merry Christmas from Georgia is my gift to those who love the holidays and entertaining. You will find recipes that are easy to prepare and a joy to share with those you love. My hope is that you will enjoy using this cookbook in celebrating this wonderful time of year.

Merry Christmas from Georgia is a collection of recipes that reflect the wonderful flavors of Georgia and the South. To those who contributed their recipes, thank you for sharing your favorite dishes with us. The Gift Giving Goody section is my personal favorite because the recipes are ones that come from the heart, so enjoy and have a wonderful holiday!

Merry Christmas to you!

Michelle Stone

Table of Contents

Appetizers

Seafood Delight Spread

8 ounces cream cheese, softened
6 ounces crab meat, drained and flaked
½ cup seafood sauce
¼ cup prepared horseradish
1 teaspoon lemon juice

Beat cream cheese until smooth. Spread onto a serving plate. Combine crab meat, seafood sauce, horseradish and lemon juice; mix well. Spread over cream cheese. Serve with crackers. Makes 2 cups.

Holly Jolly Artichoke Dip

1 can artichoke hearts
1 cup mayonnaise
1½ cups shredded Mozzarella cheese
1 cup Parmesan cheese
1 jalapeño pepper, chopped

Mix all ingredients and bake at 350 degrees for 20 minutes or until bubbly and cheese begins to brown. Serve on assorted crackers.

Festive Taco Dip

16-ounce can refried beans
8 ounces cream cheese, softened
1 cup sour cream
2 tablespoons taco seasoning
2 garlic cloves, pressed
2 ounces shredded Cheddar cheese
¼ cup chopped olives
2 tablespoons cilantro or parsley
1 tablespoon Southwestern seasoning
1 medium tomato, seeded and chopped
¼ cup thinly sliced green onions including tops

Preheat oven to 350 degrees. Spread refried beans over bottom of 2-quart baking dish. Combine cream cheese, sour cream and taco seasoning. Add garlic; mix well. Spread over beans. Add cheese to top. Bake 15 to 18 minutes or until hot. Sprinkle olives, cilantro, Southwestern seasoning, tomato and onions over dip. Garnish with additional sour cream. Serve with baked tortilla chips.

Bright and Easy Bacon and Cheese Dip

1 pound shredded Cheddar cheese
16 slices cooked bacon, crumbled
1 cup toasted almonds, chopped
2 cups mayonnaise

Mix all ingredients and refrigerate until ready to serve. Great addition to raw vegetables or assorted crackers.

Sledder's Sausage Dip

2 pounds Velveeta, cubed
2 cans Rotel tomatoes
2 pounds ground sausage, cooked and drained
1 cup chopped green onions

Place all ingredients in crock pot. Cook on low until cheese is melted. Serve with tortilla chips or crackers.

New Year's Confetti Dip

1 package onion soup mix
1 pint sour cream
¼ cup finely chopped pared cucumber
¼ cup finely chopped green pepper
¼ cup finely diced pimento

Combine all ingredients. Chill at least an hour. Serve as a dip with crackers. Makes 2¼ cups.

Christmas Party Cucumber Dip

1 medium cucumber
1 clove garlic, finely chopped
3 scallions, finely chopped
1 teaspoon olive oil
½ teaspoon vinegar
1 teaspoon dill weed
1 cup plain yogurt

Peel cucumber, cut in half lengthwise and scoop out seeds and discard them. Chop cucumber into small chunks. Mix cucumber with remaining ingredients, adding yogurt last. Stir gently to combine. Cover and chill at least 2 hours for flavors to blend. Garnish with tomatoes if desired. Makes 1½ cups.

Favorite Cheese Ball

16 ounces cream cheese, softened
8 ounces shredded sharp Cheddar cheese
½ cup grated Parmesan cheese
½ cup salad dressing
¼ cup chopped green onions
¼ teaspoon black pepper or ground red pepper
1 cup chopped pecans
Pimento or red pepper, cut into strips

Beat cheeses and dressing with electric mixer on medium speed until well blended. Add onions and pepper; mix well. Refrigerate several hours or overnight. Shape into ball; roll in pecans. Garnish with pimento or red pepper strips.

May substitute finely chopped parsley, walnuts or toasted chopped almonds for pecans.

North Pole Salmon Ball

1 large can red salmon
8 ounces cream cheese, softened
1 tablespoon lemon juice
1 teaspoon dried onion
1 teaspoon horseradish
¼ teaspoon salt
¼ teaspoon liquid smoke
Chopped pecans

Drain salmon and mix all ingredients except pecans until well blended. Refrigerate. When ready to serve, shape into ball and roll in pecans. Serve with crackers.

Feliz Navidad Snack Squares

2 tablespoons cornmeal
Two 8-ounce packages refrigerated crescent rolls
16-ounce can refried beans
2 tablespoons Southwestern seasoning
1½ cups shredded sharp Cheddar cheese
1 medium tomato, chopped
2 green onions including tops, sliced
¼ cup chopped olives
1 cup salsa
Sour cream

Preheat oven to 350 degrees. Sprinkle 9 x 13-inch baking dish with cornmeal. Unroll crescent rolls; place longest sides of dough over shortest sides of pan. Press perforations to seal; roll dough slightly up sides of pan. Bake 18 to 20 minutes or until golden brown. Cool completely. Combine refried beans and seasoning; spread over crust. Add cheese to top. Sprinkle vegetables over cheese. Cut and top each serving with salsa and sour cream.

Sensational Sausage Appetizer

1 pound pork sausage
½ pound chopped, fresh mushrooms
1 pound Velveeta, cubed
3 tablespoons creamy Italian dressing
Seasonings to taste

Brown sausage and drain. Sauté mushrooms, drain and add to sausage. Melt cheese and stir along with dressing into meat mixture. Season to taste. Place mixture on party rye bread slices and broil in oven until brown. Serve hot.

Decorative Sausage Pinwheels

2 cups biscuit mix
½ cup milk
¼ cup butter or margarine, melted
1 pound sausage

Combine biscuit mix, milk and butter and stir until blended. Refrigerate 30 minutes. Divide into two portions. Roll out one portion on floured surface to ⅛-inch thick rectangle. Spread with half the sausage. Roll lengthwise into long roll. Repeat with remaining dough and sausage. Place rolls in freezer until can be cut easily. Cut rolls into thin slices. Place on baking sheets. Bake at 400 degrees for 15 minutes. Makes 48 pinwheels.

Delicious Crab Rangoon

8 ounces flaked or imitation crab meat
8-ounce package cream cheese, softened
Dash of Worcestershire sauce
2 thinly sliced green onions
1 teaspoon lemon juice
Pinch of garlic powder
1 package wonton wrappers
Bowl of water, to dip your fingers

Mix the crab meat, cream cheese, Worcestershire sauce, green onions, lemon juice and garlic powder with a fork. Mix well. Set in refrigerator for flavors to mix. Spoon a teaspoon sized amount of the mixture into the middle of a single wonton wrapper. Dip finger into water and apply to edges of the wrapper. Fold in half to seal like a tiny purse.

Deep fry for 2 to 3 minutes or until the skins turn golden brown. Boil if desired. When they come to the top of the boiling water they're done. If you want to steam, place them in a ventilated pan about 1 inch apart. Steam for 5 minutes.

To freeze: place on a cookie sheet and make sure they aren't touching. Freeze until solid and store in a plastic bag. Thaw before cooking.

Happy Holiday Meatballs

2½ cups minced cooked chicken breast
3 tablespoons finely chopped onion
3 tablespoons finely chopped celery
2 tablespoons finely chopped carrot
2 tablespoons dry bread crumbs
1 egg white
½ teaspoon poultry seasoning
Pinch of pepper

Combine all ingredients; mix well. Shape into ¾-inch balls; place on cookie sheet. Bake at 400 degrees for 8 to 10 minutes or until lightly brown. Makes 2½ dozen. Serve with your favorite dipping sauce.

Office Party Vegetable Pizza

2 cans refrigerated crescent rolls
16 ounces cream cheese
1 cup mayonnaise
1 package ranch dressing mix
Cauliflower, chopped
Onion, chopped
Green pepper, chopped
Broccoli, chopped
Tomato, chopped
Grated Cheddar cheese

Spread crescent rolls out in rectangle on cookie sheet. Bake at 350 degrees for 10 minutes or until brown; cool. Beat cream cheese, mayonnaise and dressing mix; spread over crust. Top with chopped vegetables and cheese. Cut into squares and serve.

Merry Mini Cheeseburgers

1 pound ground beef
1 pound Velveeta, cubed
1 package dry onion soup mix
Dill pickle slices
2 can refrigerated crescent rolls

Brown grown beef; drain. Stir in cheese and soup. Cut crescent rolls in half making 16 from each can. Spoon mound of beef mixture on each crescent. Add pickle. Fold over and seal. Bake for 20 minutes at 350 degrees. May be frozen and reheated.

Beverages

Peppermint Eggnog Punch

1 quart mint ice cream, softened
1 quart eggnog
1 cup rum
48 ounces ginger ale, chilled
Candy canes

Reserve 3 scoops of ice cream for garnish. Stir together remaining ice cream, eggnog and rum. Transfer to punch bowl and add ginger ale. Place ice cream scoops in punch bowl. Garnish each glass with a candy cane.

Mock Champagne

1 quart apple juice
2 large bottles ginger ale
Few drops red food coloring
Frozen ice cubes with red cherries, green cherries
or mint leaves frozen inside

Mix apple juice and ginger ale, adding food coloring to make beverage a light pink. Put ice cubes in glasses and add beverage.

Perfect Party Punch

½ cup tropical punch or lemonade sweetened Kool-Aid
6 cups cold water and ice cubes
2 cups chilled mango nectar or apricot nectar
1 cup chilled orange juice

Place drink mix in large pitcher or punch bowl. Add water and ice cubes; stir to dissolve. Stir in nectar and orange juice. Refrigerate until ready to serve. Makes 10 servings.

Hostess Punch à la Colada

1 large can unsweetened pineapple juice
1 large can orange juice
1 can cream of coconut
1 can pina colada mix
1 bottle ginger ale, chilled

Mix all ingredients and serve over ice.

Celebration Punch

Three 24-ounce bottles white grape juice
48 ounces pineapple juice
6-ounce package frozen lemonade concentrate, thawed
½ cup sugar
12 cinnamon sticks, broken
4 teaspoons whole cloves
2 teaspoons whole allspice
Rind of one lemon, cut into strips

Pour juices into 24 cup electric percolator; add sugar. Place spices and rind in basket and percolate.

St. Nick's Slush

1½ cups sugar
2 cups hot water
Two 12-ounce cans frozen orange juice, thawed
1 large jar maraschino cherries
1 can pineapple
1 large container frozen strawberries, thawed
6 bananas, mashed

Mix together sugar and water. Dilute orange juice as directed. Cut up cherries. Mix ingredients together and freeze. Take out 3 to 4 hours before serving.

Great Tea for Brunch

7 regular tea bags
1½ cups water
Sugar, to taste
12-ounce package frozen orange juice concentrate, thawed
12-ounce package frozen lemonade concentrate, thawed

Brew tea and water. Remove tea bags and add sugar; stir until dissolved. Add juices. Fill container to top with water. Refrigerate until ready to serve.

Plantation Tea

1 gallon unsweetened tea
1 package lemonade Kool-Aid
2½ cups sugar
¾ cup white grape juice

Combine ingredients and refrigerate until ready to serve.

Hospitality Tea

2 quarts water
6 regular tea bags
8-ounce jar maraschino cherries, undrained
½ cup water
1 cup sugar
1½ cups lemon juice
2½ cups pineapple juice
Lemon slices
Mint sprigs

Bring water to a boil and pour over tea bags. Cover and let stand 5 minutes; discard tea bags. Drain cherries, reserving juice. Combine ½ cup water and sugar; boil 5 minutes. Add sugar mixture, lemon juice, pineapple juice and cherry juice to tea. Garnish with lemon slices, mint sprigs and maraschino cherries. Serve hot or cold.

Frosty Eve Hot Chocolate

1 cup water
2 squares unsweetened baking chocolate
½ cup sugar
3 cups milk
1 teaspoon vanilla

Heat water and chocolate in 2-quart saucepan on low heat. Stir constantly with wire whisk until chocolate is melted and mixture is blended. Add sugar; increase heat to medium-high. Bring to a boil and continue boiling for 3 minutes, whisking constantly. Gradually whisk in milk and vanilla. Continue on medium heat until heated through. Garnish with candy cane and marshmallows.

Cozy Hot Chocolate

1½ cups milk
1 tablespoon cocoa
1 tablespoon sugar
3 tablespoons whipping cream
1 to 2 caps almond extract
3 to 7 mini marshmallows

Heat milk in microwave for 2 minutes on high. Put cocoa and sugar into cup and add whipping cream. Stir until smooth. Add heated milk and almond extract, then stir. Add marshmallows and enjoy.

Warm You Up Coffee

½ cup ground coffee
1 tablespoon cinnamon
¼ teaspoon nutmeg
5 cups cold water
¼ cup brown sugar
⅓ cup chocolate syrup
1 cup milk
1 teaspoon vanilla

Place coffee, cinnamon, and nutmeg in a coffee filter, brew with water. Mix brown sugar, chocolate syrup, and milk; cook and simmer until brown sugar is dissolved. Add coffee and vanilla to above mixture. May be served with cream.

Can be doubled as it can be stored in a closed container in the refrigerator, and heated by the cupful in the microwave.

Coffeeblanca

2 tablespoons instant coffee granules
¼ cup water
2 cups milk
1 pint vanilla ice cream, softened
3 tablespoons chocolate syrup
1 tablespoon vanilla extract
½ cup coffee liqueur

Stir together first 3 ingredients until instant coffee dissolves. Pour into 2 ice cube trays; freeze until firm. Process cubes, ice cream, chocolate syrup, vanilla and liqueur in a blender until smooth; serve immediately. Makes 6 cups.

Hot Buttered Cranberry Punch

2 cups water
4 cups cranberries
1½ cups water
⅔ cup firmly packed brown sugar
½ teaspoon ground cinnamon
¼ teaspoon ground allspice
¼ teaspoon ground cloves
⅛ teaspoon ground nutmeg
⅛ teaspoon salt
2¼ cups unsweetened pineapple juice
Butter or margarine

Bring 2 cups water to a boil; add cranberries. Cook, uncovered until skins pop. Blend cranberries to make puree. Bring 1½ cups water, brown sugar and spices to a boil; add cranberry puree and pineapple juice. Return to heat; simmer for 5 minutes. Pour into cups or mugs; dot with butter. Serve with cinnamon stick stirrers. Makes 1½ quarts.

Breads

Peach State Bread

32-ounce can peach slices
1 cup sugar
½ cup shortening
2 eggs
2 cups flour
1 teaspoon baking soda
1 teaspoon baking powder
¼ teaspoon salt
1½ teaspoons vanilla
½ cup finely chopped pecans
1 teaspoon cinnamon

Drain peaches, saving syrup. Chop into fine pieces. Cream together sugar with shortening. Add eggs and continue to mix. Gradually fold in dry ingredients, except cinnamon. Using a wooden spoon, fold in vanilla and pecans. Stir in chopped peaches. Pour into greased 8-inch square pan or 9 x 5-inch loaf pan. Sprinkle with the cinnamon. Bake at 325 degrees for 1 hour 5 minutes. Cool 20 minutes before removing from pan.

The Great Pumpkin Bread

½ cup butter or margarine, softened
1 cup firmly packed brown sugar
2 large eggs
2 cups all-purpose flour
2 teaspoons baking powder
¼ teaspoon baking soda
½ teaspoon salt
2 teaspoons pumpkin pie spice
1 cup mashed, cooked pumpkin
½ cup chopped pecans, toasted
1 teaspoon vanilla
Peachy Cream Cheese Spread

Beat butter at medium speed until creamy; gradually add brown sugar, beating well. Add eggs, 1 at a time, beating until blended after each addition. Combine flour and next 4 ingredients; add to butter mixture alternately with pumpkin, beginning and ending with flour mixture. Beat at low speed after each addition, just until dry ingredients are moistened. Stir chopped pecans and vanilla into batter. Spoon into a greased 8½ x 4½-inch loaf pan. Bake at 350 degrees for 1 hour or until a wooden pick inserted in center comes out clean. Cool in pan 10 minutes; remove from pan, and cool until ready to serve. Makes 1 loaf. Slice and serve with Peachy Cream Cheese Spread.

Peachy Cream Cheese Spread

8-ounce package cream cheese, softened
⅓ cup peach preserves
¼ teaspoon ground ginger

Beat all ingredients at low speed until blended. Makes 1⅓ cups.

Georgia Pecan Loaf

¾ cup brown sugar
¼ cup shortening
1 egg
2 cups sifted all-purpose flour
1 teaspoon baking soda
½ teaspoon salt
⅓ cup frozen orange juice concentrate, thawed
One 8¾-ounce can crushed pineapple
½ cup chopped pecans

Cream together brown sugar and shortening. Add egg. Beat well. Sift together flour, baking soda and salt. Alternately add the dry ingredients and orange concentrate to creamed mixture, stirring after each addition. Stir in undrained pineapple and chopped pecans. Bake in a well-greased 8½ x 4½ x 2½-inch loaf pan at 350 degrees for 50 to 60 minutes.

Deck the Halls Breadsticks

One 11-ounce can refrigerated breadsticks, separated and cut in half
3 tablespoons butter or margarine, melted
¾ cup grated Parmesan cheese

Dip breadsticks in butter. Coat with cheese. Twist and place on ungreased cookie sheet. Bake at 350 degrees for 14 to 18 minutes or until golden brown. Makes 16 servings.

Glorious Garlic Bread

½ cup shredded Romano cheese
⅓ cup butter or margarine, softened
1 garlic clove, minced
1 teaspoon chopped rosemary
1 loaf French or Italian bread, cut in half lengthwise

Preheat oven to 400 degrees. Mix cheese, butter, garlic and rosemary. Spread on cut surfaces of bread. Place on cookie sheet and bake for 8 to 10 minutes or until lightly browned. Makes 12 servings.

Soulful Cornbread Muffins

2 cups yellow cornmeal
½ cup flour
1½ teaspoons baking powder
2 eggs
1 cup salad dressing
½ teaspoon ground red pepper
8¾-ounce can whole kernel corn, drained
½ cup chopped onion
¼ cup chopped red or green pepper

Mix cornmeal, flour and baking powder in large bowl. Beat eggs in small bowl; stir in salad dressing and pepper. Add to flour mixture; stir just until moistened. Stir in remaining ingredients. Spoon batter into greased muffin tins, filling each ⅔ full. Bake at 400 degrees for 30 minutes. Makes 12 servings.

Cheddar Garlic Biscuits

2 cups biscuit mix
½ cup grated Cheddar cheese
⅔ cup milk
½ cup melted butter
¼ teaspoon garlic powder

Mix biscuit mix, cheese and milk. Drop by spoonfuls onto greased cookie sheet. Bake at 400 degrees until brown. Mix butter and garlic powder; brush tops of biscuits when done.

Angelic Mayonnaise Rolls

1 cup self-rising flour
½ cup milk
2 tablespoons mayonnaise

Combine all ingredients and mix well. Fill greased muffin tins ⅔ full. Bake at 375 degrees for 14 minutes. Makes 6 rolls.

Jubilant Biscuits

3 cups biscuit mix
3 tablespoons sugar
One 12-ounce can beer

Mix dry ingredients first. Pour in beer and stir until blended. It does not need to be smooth. Fill greased muffin tins ½ full. Bake at 400 degrees for 15 minutes. Serves 8.

Crystal Palace Rolls

2 packages active dry yeast
1¾ cups warm water
2 eggs
½ cup sugar
¼ cup butter or margarine, softened
1 teaspoon salt
6 cups all-purpose flour, divided

Dissolve yeast in water. Add eggs, sugar, butter, salt and 3 cups of flour; beat until smooth. Add enough of remaining flour to form a soft dough. Turn onto a floured surface and knead until smooth and elastic. Place in a greased bowl, turning once to coat. Cover and refrigerate for 2 hours or up to 2 days. Punch dough down and divide in half; shape each half into 12 rolls. Place in 2 greased 9-inch round baking pans. Cover and let rise until nearly doubled. Bake at 350 degrees for 20 minutes or until golden brown. Makes 2 dozen.

Yuletide Yogurt Biscuits

1 cup plus 2 tablespoons all-purpose flour
1½ teaspoons baking powder
½ teaspoon salt
¼ teaspoon baking soda
2 tablespoons cold butter or margarine
½ cup plain yogurt
1 teaspoon sugar
½ teaspoon milk

Combine flour, baking powder, salt and baking soda; cut in butter until crumbly. Combine yogurt and sugar; stir into dry ingredients just until moistened. Turn onto a floured surface; knead 4 to 5 times. Place on a greased baking sheet; pat into a 6 x 4-inch rectangle. Cut into six square biscuits, not separating biscuits. Brush tops with milk. Bake at 450 degrees for 12 to 15 minutes. Makes 6 biscuits.

Breakfast & Brunch

Overnight Guests Cinnamon Pull Apart

¾ cup chopped pecans
24 frozen rolls
½ cup butter
1 teaspoon cinnamon
1 cup brown sugar
4-ounce package instant butterscotch pudding

Coat bundt pan with spray. Place pecans in bottom of pan and add frozen bread rolls. Melt butter and stir in cinnamon and sugar until dissolved. Sprinkle pudding mix over rolls. Pour butter mixture over all. Set in cold oven overnight. Bake at 350 degrees for about 30 minutes. While hot turn out onto serving platter.

New Year's Morning Cheese Danish

1 egg, separated
1 teaspoon vanilla
½ cup sugar
8 ounces cream cheese
¼ cup peach jam
Two 10-ounce cans refrigerated crescent rolls

Mix egg yolk, vanilla, sugar, and cream cheese. On a greased cookie sheet, roll out 1 can of crescent rolls. Spread jam on top of dough. Cover with egg mixture. Press out remaining can of rolls on top of mixture. Seal edges with fingertips. Whip egg white and spread on top. Bake at 350 degrees for 20 minutes. Cut and serve warm.

Early Riser's French Toast Fingers

2 eggs
¼ cup milk
¼ teaspoon salt
½ cup peach preserves
8 slices day-old white bread
Powdered sugar

Beat eggs, milk and salt; set aside. Spread preserves on four slices of bread; top with remaining slices. Trim crusts; Cut each into three strips. Dip both sides in egg mixture. Cook on a lightly greased griddle for 2 minutes on each side. Dust with powdered sugar. Makes 4 servings.

Best French Toast

6 eggs
1 cup milk
1 teaspoon salt
⅔ cup vegetable oil
1 teaspoon vanilla
½ cup sugar
1 teaspoon nutmeg
1 teaspoon cinnamon
8 slices bread, sliced 1-inch thick

Combine all ingredients except bread. Place bread in a greased baking dish and pour egg mixture over. Cover and refrigerate overnight. Bake at 450 degrees for 10 minutes; turn and bake 10 minutes more.

Good Morning Lemon Muffins

½ cup butter or margarine, softened
½ cup sugar
2 eggs, separated
1 cup all-purpose flour
1 teaspoon baking powder
¼ teaspoon salt
3 tablespoons lemon juice
1 tablespoon grated lemon peel
Cinnamon-sugar

Cream butter and sugar. Add egg yolks; mix well. Combine flour, baking powder and salt; add alternately with lemon juice to the creamed mixture. Beat egg whites until stiff peaks form; fold into batter with lemon peel. Fill greased or paper lined muffin tins ⅔ full. Sprinkle with cinnamon-sugar. Bake at 350 degrees for 20 to 25 minutes or until toothpick inserted comes out clean. Makes 9 muffins.

Apple Bran Muffins

1¼ cups bran cereal
½ cup skim milk
1 cup flour
1½ teaspoons baking powder
¼ teaspoon ground cinnamon
¼ teaspoon salt
⅓ cup vegetable oil spread
¼ cup sugar
1 egg
½ cup chopped apple

Mix cereal and milk; let stand 5 minutes or until softened. Mix flour, baking powder, cinnamon and salt. Beat spread and sugar until light and fluffy. Blend in cereal mixture and add egg. Add to flour mixture, mixing just until moistened. Stir in apple. Spoon batter into greased muffin tins, filling each ⅔ full. Bake at 400 degrees for 25 to 30 minutes or until golden brown. Makes 6 muffins.

Cranberry Raisin Muffins

2 cups raisin bran cereal
1 cup skim milk
½ cup brown sugar
1¼ cups self-rising flour
½ teaspoon soda
½ teaspoon cinnamon
½ small container plain yogurt
⅓ cup whole cranberry sauce

Mix cereal and milk and let stand. Mix sugar, flour, soda, cinnamon; add cereal and mix. Blend in yogurt and cranberry sauce. Bake at 400 degrees for 20 minutes. Makes 12 muffins.

Orange Delight Muffins

Two 6-ounce cans frozen orange juice concentrate, thawed
½ cup sugar
4 tablespoons oil
2 eggs, beaten
4 cups biscuit mix
1 cup orange marmalade
1 cup granola or chopped, toasted pecans

Combine juice, sugar, oil and eggs. Add biscuit mix, marmalade and nuts. Pour into 12 greased muffin tins and bake at 400 degrees for 20 minutes.

Banana Pecan Muffins

1 box banana cake mix
1 small banana, mashed
½ cup chopped pecans
3 eggs
⅓ cup oil
1 cup water

Preheat oven to 350 degrees. Grease and flour muffin pan. Combine all ingredients; mix until well blended. Spoon into muffin cups, filling ¾ full. Bake for 20 to 25 minutes or until toothpick inserted comes out clean. Completely cool before serving. Makes 12 muffins.

Six Weeks Bran Muffins

15-ounce box raisin bran cereal
5 cups flour
4 eggs
3 cups sugar
1 quart buttermilk
5 teaspoons soda
2 teaspoons salt

Mix all ingredients well. Store in an airtight container in refrigerator up to six weeks. May spoon out as needed. Bake at 400 degrees for 15 minutes.

Add ½ teaspoon of your favorite jam to each muffin cup before baking for a nice surprise.

Winter Breakfast Dish

2½ cups seasoned croutons
2 cups shredded Cheddar cheese
2 pounds sausage
4 eggs
¾ teaspoon dry mustard
2½ cups milk
1 cup mushroom soup
1 small can mushrooms

Place croutons in bottom of greased 8 x 8-inch baking dish. Top with cheese. Cook sausage; drain. Place sausage over cheese. Beat together eggs, mustard, milk, mushroom soup and mushrooms. Pour over sausage. Bake at 300 degrees for 1 hour 30 minutes.

Can be prepared ahead and refrigerated before cooking.

Brunch Torte

2 frozen pie crusts, thawed
1 cup shredded Cheddar cheese
¾ pound thinly sliced cooked ham
1½ cups thinly sliced, unpeeled red potatoes
1 medium onion, sliced
9 ounces frozen spinach, thawed and squeezed to drain
1 egg
1 tablespoon water

Preheat oven to 375 degrees. Put cookie sheet in oven to heat. Press one crust on bottom and up sides of a 9-inch pie pan. Sprinkle ⅓ cup cheese on bottom of crust. Top with half of ham, half of potatoes and half of onion slices. Distribute spinach evenly over onion. Top with ⅓ cup cheese and remaining ham, potatoes and onion. Sprinkle remaining cheese over onion. Gently press mixture into pan. Top with second crust; fold over top edge of bottom crust and pinch edges to seal. Cut slits in top crust. Mix egg and water and brush top with mixture. Place torte on hot cookie sheet and bake at 375 degrees for 45 to 60 minutes or until crust is golden brown and filling is thoroughly heated. Makes 8 servings.

Artichoke Quiche

9-inch pastry shell
2 tablespoons butter
⅓ cup chopped green onion
2 eggs
1 tablespoon flour
⅔ cup cream
14-ounce can artichoke hearts, well drained and coarsely chopped
1 cup grated hot pepper cheese
1 cup grated Cheddar cheese

Bake pastry shell according to directions for 12 minutes. Remove from oven and reduce to 350 degrees. Melt butter; sauté onion. Beat eggs, flour and cream together. Stir in artichoke hearts, hot pepper cheese, Cheddar cheese and onions. Reserve 3 tablespoons Cheddar for top. Stir until well blended. Pour into shell and bake for 45 minutes or until firm in center. Sprinkle reserved cheese on top in last 10 minutes of cooking time. Makes 6 servings.

Christmas Morning Casserole

½ cup chopped onion
2 tablespoons butter
2 tablespoons flour
1¼ cups milk
1 cup shredded, sharp Cheddar cheese
6 hard cooked eggs, sliced
1½ cups crushed potato chips
10 slices bacon, fried crisp and crumbled

Cook onion in butter until tender and blend in flour. Add milk and cook until thickens. Add cheese and stir until cheese is melted. Place layer of egg slices in a 10 x 6-inch baking dish. Cover with half of cheese sauce, half of potato chips and half of bacon. Repeat with a second layer. Bake at 350 degrees about 30 minutes.

Soups & Salads

Winter Squash Soup

12-ounce package frozen squash
14½-ounce can chicken broth
1 cup sliced carrots
⅓ cup chopped onion
¼ teaspoon dried basil leaves, crushed
¾ cup salad dressing, divided
1 tablespoon milk

Combine all ingredients except salad dressing and milk in a saucepan. Bring to a boil; cover. Reduce heat to medium; simmer 12 to 15 minutes or until carrots and onions are tender. Whisk in ½ cup salad dressing; heat thoroughly, stirring occasionally. Mix remaining ¼ cup salad dressing and milk in a separate bowl. Spoon into individual serving bowls. Top with salad dressing mixture; swirl gently with spoon. Makes 4 servings.

Coastal Georgia Clam Chowder

1 stick butter
1 onion, chopped
3 small cans New England clam chowder soup
5 small cans cream of potato soup
2 to 4 cans minced clams
½ gallon half-and-half

Sauté onion in butter. Add ingredients to stock pot; bring to a boil, stirring constantly. Reduce heat to low and simmer for 30 minutes. Serves 12.

Southern Cream of Pecan Soup

2 tablespoons butter
3 tablespoons finely chopped onion
1 tablespoon all-purpose flour
2 cups chicken stock or broth
½ teaspoon salt
Freshly ground pepper
1 cup finely ground pecans
1 small sprig celery leaves
1½ cups light cream or half-and-half
4 small sprigs mint

Melt butter in heavy saucepan over medium heat. Add onion and sauté. Stir in flour; cook, stirring, over low heat 1 minute. Gradually pour in stock, stirring constantly. Stir in salt and pepper to taste. Add pecans and sprig of celery leaves. Increase heat to medium; heat soup to boiling. Reduce heat to low. Simmer 10 minutes, stirring occasionally. Stir in cream; simmer over very low heat 5 minutes. Ladle into individual warmed bowls. Top with a sprig of mint. Serve at once. Serves 4.

Fabulous Cream of Vegetable Soup

2 tablespoons butter
1 clove garlic, chopped
1 medium onion, sliced
¼ head of cauliflower, broken
2 carrots, chopped
2 stalks celery, chopped
6 asparagus stalks, chopped
1 leek, chopped
1 large potato, peeled and chopped
1 cup chopped spinach
Salt and pepper, to taste
1 quart chicken stock
Pinch of cayenne pepper
1 cup heavy cream
3 tablespoons flour
1 tablespoon chopped parsley
1 tablespoon Parmesan cheese

Heat butter in a soup pot; add onion and garlic and sauté for 3 minutes. Add vegetables to the pot and cook 5 to 6 minutes. Add the chicken stock and simmer 25 to 30 minutes. Mix the cream and flour until smooth. Pour slowly into the soup, stirring constantly. Simmer until begins thickening. Serve with parsley and grated Parmesan cheese on top.

White Christmas Chili

16 ounces white beans, uncooked
3 to 4 chicken breasts, uncooked
1 large can chicken broth
1 onion, chopped
2 cloves garlic
Chili powder, to taste or package of chili seasoning
1 can cream of mushroom soup
Salt and pepper, to taste

Place all ingredients except soup in crock pot. Cook on high all day and beans and chicken will cook. Before serving tear chicken apart with fork and add soup; season to taste. Allow to heat thoroughly and serve.

Steak and Spinach Salad

⅓ cup vinegar
1 envelope Parmesan Italian salad dressing mix
⅓ cup olive oil
1 garlic clove, minced
One 1-pound beef sirloin steak, ½ to ¾-inch thick
8 cups torn spinach
1 cup sliced mushrooms
1 large tomato, cut into wedges
¼ cup sliced green onions

Mix vinegar, salad dressing mix, oil and garlic.   Mix until well blended. Reserve ⅓ cup dressing; refrigerate. Pour remaining dressing over steak; cover. Refrigerate at least 1 hour. Drain; discard dressing. Grill or broil as desired. Cut into slices. Toss spinach, mushrooms, tomato and onions with reserved dressing. Arrange steak slices over salad. Makes 4 servings.

New Year's Day Black-Eyed Pea Salad

2 large cans black-eyed peas, drained
⅔ cup red wine vinegar
1 cup chopped onion
1 tablespoon pepper
1½ cups salad oil
Dash of garlic powder
1 large can of chopped mushrooms, drained

Bring black-eyed peas to a boil; season with butter, salt and pepper. Cool and add remaining ingredients. Toss and serve.

Broccoli Salad

½ cup mayonnaise
½ cup sugar
2 tablespoons apple cider vinegar
2 heads broccoli, chopped
½ cup raisins
½ cup chopped red onion
½ cup pecans
12 slices crumbled bacon

Mix mayonnaise, sugar and vinegar until well blended. Refrigerate overnight. Mix broccoli, raisins, onion and pecans together. Pour dressing over and top with crumbled bacon.

Macaroni Salad

One 7¼-ounce package macaroni
3 hard cooked eggs, chopped
¾ cup mayonnaise
1 small red pepper, chopped
1 small green pepper, chopped
1 small onion, finely chopped
Black pepper, to taste

Prepare macaroni as directed on package. Add eggs, mayonnaise, peppers and onion; mix well. Season to taste with pepper. Refrigerate until ready to serve. Add additional mayonnaise before serving, if desired. Makes 6 servings.

Fresh Mozzarella and Tomato Pasta

2 pounds tomatoes, coarsely chopped
1 envelope Italian salad dressing mix
2 tablespoons olive oil
2 tablespoons balsamic vinegar
1 pound pasta, cooked and drained
9 ounces shredded Mozzarella cheese
¼ cup chopped basil
Salt and black pepper, to taste

Mix tomatoes, salad dressing mix, olive oil and vinegar until well blended. Add pasta, Mozzarella and basil; toss to mix well. Season to taste. Cover and refrigerate until ready to serve.

Mixed Vegetable Salad

¾ cup white vinegar
½ cup vegetable oil
1 cup sugar
1 teaspoon salt
1 teaspoon pepper
1 can whole kernel corn, drained
1 can peas, drained
1 can green beans, drained
1 cup diced bell pepper
1 cup diced celery
1 cup chopped onion
1 cup shredded carrots

Bring first 5 ingredients to a boil, stirring until sugar dissolves. Cool. Add remaining ingredients. Chill 8 hours or overnight.

Any vegetables may be substituted and can size is also a matter of preference.

Traditional Cranberry Salad

2 cups whole cranberry sauce
2 cup boiling water
6 ounces cherry or raspberry gelatin
½ cup cold water
½ cup orange juice
Rind of one orange
¼ cup sugar
1 cup pecans
1 large apple, peeled and chopped

Soften cranberry sauce in boiling water. Add remaining ingredients and refrigerate to set. Stir once after partially set.

Side Items

Ring in the New Year Cabbage Casserole

1 medium cabbage, chopped
10 ounces cream of celery soup
8 ounces sliced water chestnuts
½ cup salad dressing
½ cup toasted pecans
8 ounces stuffing mix
¾ cup grated Cheddar cheese

Boil cabbage until tender. Drain. Mix soup, water chestnuts and salad dressing with drained cabbage. Place in a buttered casserole dish. Top with pecans which have been mixed with stuffing mix. Sprinkle with cheese. Bake at 350 degrees until bubbly.

Curried Mashed Sweet Potatoes

1½ pounds sweet potatoes, peeled and quartered
1 tablespoon olive oil
1 medium onion, finely chopped
2 teaspoons curry powder
½ cup sour cream
½ teaspoon salt

Cook sweet potatoes in boiling water for 15 minutes or until tender. Drain. Meanwhile heat oil on medium-high heat. Add onion; cook and stir 4 minutes. Add curry powder; cook an additional 2 minutes, stirring frequently. Remove from heat. Mash cooked sweet potatoes. Stir in onion mixture, sour cream and salt. Serve immediately. Makes 6 servings.

Sensational Sautéed Mushrooms

1 tablespoon olive oil
3 tablespoons butter
16 to 18 ounces mushrooms, washed and sliced
3 tablespoons Worcestershire sauce
1½ tablespoons soy sauce
Seasoned salt, to taste
Garlic powder, to taste
Black pepper, to taste
4 to 5 drops hot sauce

Heat olive oil and butter. Add mushrooms. Add remaining ingredients and stir. Cook on low for 15 to 20 minutes.

Angelic Asparagus

1 can cream of chicken soup
½ cup milk
10-ounce package frozen cut green beans, thawed
8-ounce package frozen asparagus, thawed and drained
4-ounce can mushrooms, drained
2 cups cubed day-old bread
2 tablespoons sliced almonds
2 tablespoons butter or margarine, melted

Combine soup and milk. Add beans, asparagus and mushrooms; mix well. Pour into greased 8-inch baking dish. Cover and bake at 350 degrees for 20 minutes. Toss bread cubes, almonds and butter; sprinkle over casserole. Bake 15 to 20 minutes longer. Makes 6 to 8 servings.

Peas Amandine

16-ounces frozen peas
¼ cup slivered almonds
3 tablespoons butter or margarine
4½ ounces sliced mushrooms, drained
¼ cup chopped onion
¼ teaspoon salt
⅛ teaspoon pepper

Cook peas according to package directions; drain. Set aside. Sauté almonds in butter until lightly browned. Remove and add to peas. Sauté mushrooms and onion; add to peas. Season with salt and pepper. Makes 8 servings.

Green Bean Bundles

2 can whole green beans, drained
Bacon
1 bottle Catalina dressing

Arrange green beans in bundles and secure with bacon. Pour dressing over and place in a glass baking dish. Bake uncovered at 350 degrees for 30 minutes.

Holiday Yams and Apples

6 yams, peeled
4 or 5 green apples
1 cup sugar
1 cup water
Juice and rind of 1 orange
¼ pound butter
3 tablespoons cornstarch

Slice yams crosswise and par boil. Peel apples, slice as for pie, but thinner. Place apples in baking dish and place yams on top. Bring sugar, water, juice, orange rind, butter and cornstarch to a boil; boiling for 1 minute. Pour sauce over yams and apples; bake at 300 degrees for 1 hour.

Country Garden Primavera

3 cups chopped zucchini
2 cups cauliflowerets
¼ cup butter or margarine
1½ cups halved cherry tomatoes
1 cup corkscrew pasta, cooked and drained
1 teaspoon dried basil leaves, crushed
8 ounces Velveeta, cut up

Cook zucchini and cauliflower in butter on medium heat until tender-crisp. Add tomatoes, pasta and basil; heat thoroughly. Add cheese; continue cooking until cheese is melted. Makes 4 servings.

For the microwave: Microwave zucchini, cauliflower and butter in 3-quart casserole dish on HIGH 4 to 6 minutes or until tender-crisp, stirring every 2 minutes. Add remaining ingredients; mix lightly. Microwave on MEDIUM 4 to 6 minutes or until cheese is melted, stirring every 2 minutes.

Speedy Ziti

2 cups tomato sauce
1 cup Ricotta cheese
16 ounces ziti, cooked and drained
6 ounces Mozzarella cheese, diced
Salt and pepper, to taste
4 ounces Mozzarella cheese, sliced
¼ cup grated Parmesan or Romano cheese

Mix tomato sauce and Ricotta. Toss ziti, tomato sauce mixture, Mozzarella and salt and pepper. Pour into lightly greased 2-quart casserole dish. Cover with Mozzarella slices; sprinkle with Parmesan cheese. Bake at 350 degrees for 15 to 20 minutes or until thoroughly heated. Makes 6 servings.

Potluck Pasta and Broccoli

½ pound spaghetti, broken in half
16-ounce package frozen broccoli cuts
1 cup Velveeta cheese sauce

Cook spaghetti as directed on package, adding broccoli during last 6 minutes of cooking time. Drain. Microwave cheese sauce as directed on label. Pour over spaghetti and broccoli. Toss until thoroughly coated. Makes 4 servings.

Southerners' Cheese Grits

1 cup grits
4 cups water
1 stick butter
One 8-ounce roll garlic cheese
2 eggs
Milk
¼ cup shredded Cheddar cheese

Cook grits in water according to package directions. Add butter and cheese to cooked grits, stirring until melted. Cool. Beat eggs and add enough milk to eggs to make 1 cup of liquid. Add egg-milk mixture to grits and pour into medium greased casserole dish. Bake at 350 degrees for 45 minutes. Sprinkle cheddar cheese on top of casserole. Serves 12.

Italian Spinach Pie

2 cups cottage cheese
10-ounce package frozen chopped spinach, thawed and drained
4 eggs, beaten
1 cup shredded Mozzarella cheese
⅓ cup grated Parmesan cheese
1 teaspoon dried oregano leaves
½ cup chopped red pepper

Mix all ingredients except red pepper. Pour into buttered 9-inch pie plate. Bake at 350 degrees for 40 minutes or until center is set. Garnish with red pepper. Makes 8 servings.

Celebration Crock Pot Dressing

1½ cups chopped onion
1½ cups chopped celery
2 sticks butter
Broth from chicken
1 large skillet of cornbread, crumbled
1 teaspoon sugar
1 teaspoon pepper
2 eggs, beaten
1 can cream of mushroom soup
1 can cream of chicken soup
1 teaspoon salt
1 teaspoon sage

Sauté onion and celery in butter. Pour broth over cornbread; mix. Add remaining ingredients. Place in crock pot and cook on high for 45 minutes to 1 hour. Reduce to low and cook 4 more hours, stirring occasionally.

Curried Fruit for Christmas

1 large can apricots
1 large can pear halves
1 large can peach halves
1 large can pineapple chunks
1 small can mandarin oranges
½ cup brown sugar
2 tablespoons corn starch
1 tablespoon margarine
1 teaspoon curry powder
Maraschino cherries
Chopped pecans

Drain and save juices from fruit. Mix 2 cups juice with brown sugar, corn-starch, margarine and curry powder. Bring to a boil. Meanwhile arrange fruit in a baking dish. Pour sauce over fruit; scatter pecans on top. Bake at 350 degrees for 45 minutes to 1 hour.

Entrées

Savory Swiss Bliss

2 pounds eye of round
1 tablespoon butter
1 envelope dry onion soup mix
½ cup bell pepper, chopped
1-pound can tomatoes, drained, reserving juice
1 can cream of mushroom soup
¼ teaspoon salt
1 tablespoon A-1 sauce
1 tablespoon cornstarch

Line a 9 x 13-inch casserole with foil. Place eye of round in pan and add butter, onion soup, pepper and tomatoes. In a jar, shake cream of mushroom soup, salt, tomato juice, A-1 sauce and cornstarch. Pour over steak and cover and seal with foil. Bake at 250 degrees for 2 hours.

Simple Stroganoff

One 1-pound boneless beef top sirloin steak, ¾-inch thick
1 cup sour cream
2 tablespoons flour
½ cup water
2 teaspoons instant beef bouillon
¼ teaspoon pepper
2 tablespoons butter or margarine
1½ cups sliced fresh mushrooms
½ cup chopped onion
1 clove garlic
2 cups hot, cooked noodles

Place meat in freezer 30 minutes to firm. Cut across into 2 x ½-inch strips. Mix sour cream and flour in small bowl. Stir in water, bouillon and pepper; set aside. Melt butter in large skillet on medium-high heat. Add ½ of the meat; cook and stir until tender. Remove. Add remaining meat and vegetables. Cook and stir until meat is done and onion is tender. Return all meat to skillet. Reduce heat to medium. Add sour cream mixture; stir constantly until bubbly. Continue cooking 1 minute. Serve over hot noodles. Makes 4 servings.

Children's Favorite Chili Mac

1 package macaroni
¼ cup margarine
¼ cup milk
½ pound ground beef, cooked and drained
1 cup tomatoes, chopped
1 teaspoon chili powder

Prepare macaroni as directed on package using margarine and milk. Stir in remaining ingredients. Simmer until thoroughly heated. Makes 4 servings.

E-Z Lasagna

32-ounce container Ricotta cheese
1 egg
28-ounce jar spaghetti sauce, divided
9 lasagna noodles, uncooked
4 cups shredded Mozzarella cheese, divided
¼ cup grated Parmesan cheese

Mix Ricotta and egg until well blended. Layer ¾ cup spaghetti sauce, 3 noodles, ½ Ricotta mixture and 1½ cups Mozzarella in 9 x 13-inch baking dish. Repeat layers once. Top with remaining noodles and sauce. Sprinkle with remaining Mozzarella and Parmesan cheeses. Cover with foil. Bake at 350 degrees for 45 minutes. Remove foil. Bake 15 minutes longer or until noodles are tender. Let stand 10 minutes before serving. Makes 8 servings.

For Meat Lasagna: Prepare as directed above, increasing sauce to 32 ounces and adding 1 pound ground beef, cooked and drained.

For Spinach Lasagna: Prepare as directed above, adding two 10-ounce packages frozen chopped spinach, ½ cup grated Parmesan cheese and ¼ to ½ teaspoon dried oregano leaves to Ricotta mixture.

For Vegetable Lasagna: Prepare as directed above, adding ¼ cup chopped basil to Ricotta mixture. Thaw, drain and chop one 16-ounce package assorted frozen vegetables. Layer ½ vegetables at a time with remaining ingredients as directed.

Welcome Home Casserole

10-ounce package refrigerated flaky biscuits
3 ounces cream cheese, softened
½ cup shredded sharp Cheddar cheese
3 tablespoons dry onion soup mix, divided
1 pound ground beef
1 can cream of mushroom soup
1 cup shredded Swiss cheese
2 eggs, beaten

Separate biscuits and press into 4-inch circles. Combine cream cheese, Cheddar cheese and 1 tablespoon onion soup mix; blend well. Spoon mixture into each biscuit and fold. Press edges to seal. Brown ground beef and 2 tablespoons onion soup mix; drain. Stir in mushroom soup, Swiss cheese and eggs. Heat until bubbly. Pour into greased 9 x 13-inch baking dish. Arrange biscuits on top. Bake at 375 degrees for 22 to 28 minutes.

Bells Ringing Beef and Mozzarella

1 pound ground beef
1 teaspoon crushed basil leaves
¼ teaspoon pepper
⅛ teaspoon garlic powder
1 can Italian tomato soup
1 can cream of mushroom soup
1¼ cups water
1½ cups shredded Mozzarella cheese, divided
4 cups cooked shell macaroni

Cook beef, basil leaves, pepper and garlic powder; drain. Stir in soups, water and 1 cup cheese. Add macaroni. Spoon mixture into 2-quart baking dish. Sprinkle top with remaining cheese. Bake at 400 degrees for 25 minutes or until hot and bubbly.

Spicy Sauce for your Meatloaf

8-ounce can tomato sauce
2 tablespoons mustard
2 tablespoons Worcestershire sauce
2 tablespoons vinegar
2 tablespoons brown sugar
½ cup water

Bring all ingredients to a boil. Pour over meatloaf, basting occasionally.

Christmas Gathering Chicken and Asparagus

1 tablespoon oil
Four 1-pound boneless skinless chicken breasts
Salt and pepper, to taste
1½ cups milk
10¾-ounce can cream of chicken soup
2 cups instant rice, uncooked
10-ounce package frozen chopped asparagus, thawed
1 cup shredded Swiss or Cheddar cheese
¼ cup toasted sliced almonds

Heat oil in large skillet on medium-high heat. Add chicken; season with salt and pepper. Cover and cook 4 minutes on each side or until cooked through. Remove chicken from skillet. Add milk and soup to skillet; stir. Bring to a boil. Stir in rice and asparagus. Top with chicken. Sprinkle with cheese and almonds and cover. Cook on low heat 5 minutes. Makes 4 servings.

Company's Coming Chicken Casserole

3 large chicken breasts
3 cups instant rice
8 ounces stuffing mix
5 cups water
10¾-ounce can cream of chicken soup
½ cup sour cream
3 tablespoons margarine, melted
3 cups shredded Cheddar cheese, divided

Preheat oven to 350 degrees. Grease 9 x 13-inch baking dish. Boil chicken breasts until done. Mix rice and stuffing together. Heat water in microwave and add to rice and stuffing mixture. Set aside. Mix together soup, sour cream and margarine. Add to rice and stuffing, mix well. Add 1 cup cheese and stir. Place chicken in pan and spread mixture on top. Top with remaining cheese. Bake for 35 to 40 minutes. Makes 10 to 12 servings.

Potluck Favorite Mexican Casserole

2 to 3 large boneless skinless chicken breasts
14 ounces Mexican blended cheeses
2 cans Mexican corn with red and green peppers, drained
2 cans French cut green beans, drained
½ cup sour cream
10¾-ounce can cream of chicken soup
Two 4.5-ounce cans chopped green chiles
1 envelope taco seasoning
20 ounces Doritos, crushed

Boil chicken breasts until done. Cool and chop chicken. Preheat oven to 375 degrees. Lightly grease 9 x 13-inch baking dish. Stir together ¾ cup of cheese, chicken, corn, green beans, sour cream, soup, chiles, taco seasoning, and ¼ of chips. Pour ½ of remaining chips in bottom of pan as crust. Set aside remaining chips. Put mixture in pan and spread evenly, top with remaining cheese and chips. Bake for 30 minutes. Makes 10 to 12 servings.

You can use 1½ pounds of fried hamburger meat instead of chicken.

Chilly Eve Chicken and Broccoli Casserole

2 to 3 large chicken breasts
16-ounce package frozen broccoli
1 teaspoon lemon juice
½ cup shredded Swiss cheese
1 cup shredded Cheddar cheese
½ cup sour cream
10¾-ounce can cream of broccoli soup
10¾-ounce can cream of chicken soup
15½ ounces Tostitos, crushed

Boil chicken breasts until done. Cool and chop chicken. Preheat of 375 degrees. Grease 9 x 13-inch baking dish. Boil broccoli for 4 to 5 minutes or until tender. Mix lemon juice, ½ of Swiss and ½ of Cheddar, sour cream, soups, chicken, broccoli, and ¼ of chips together. Pour ½ remaining chips into bottom of pan for crust. Set aside remaining chips. Pour mixture into pan and spread evenly. Top with remaining cheese and chips. Bake for 30 minutes. Makes 10 to 12 servings.

Christmas Eve Chicken Lucerne

1 chicken bouillon cube
½ cup boiling water
6 tablespoons butter or margarine, divided
¼ cup flour
¼ teaspoon dried tarragon leaves
Dash of ground red pepper
1 cup milk
8-ounce package Swiss cheese slices, cut into strips
4 whole chicken breasts, cooked
1 cup bread crumbs

Dissolve bouillon cube in water. Melt 3 tablespoons butter in saucepan on low heat. Blend in flour and seasonings. Gradually add milk and bouillon; cook, stirring constantly, until thickened. Add cheese; stir until melted. Place chicken in 8 x 12-inch baking dish; cover with sauce. Melt remaining 3 tablespoons butter; toss with crumbs. Sprinkle crumbs over chicken. Bake at 375 degrees for 20 to 25 minutes or until thoroughly heated. Makes 8 servings.

Cheesy Salsa Chicken

Four 1¼-pound boneless skinless chicken breasts, cut into chunks
1 cup salsa
½ cup water
½ pound Velveeta, cut up
1½ cups instant rice, uncooked

Spray large skillet with non stick cooking spray. Add chicken; cook and stir 4 to 5 minutes or until cooked through. Stir in salsa, water and cheese. Bring to a boil. Stir in rice; cover. Remove from heat. Let stand 7 minutes or until liquid is absorbed and rice is tender. Stir before serving. Makes 4 servings.

Chicken and Asparagus with Mushrooms

8 ounces portobella mushrooms, sliced
1 pound asparagus, cut into 2-inch pieces
1 cup balsamic vinaigrette dressing
2 tablespoons chopped sundried tomatoes
2 cups bowtie or shell pasta, cooked and drained
6 ounces precooked chicken breast strips, chopped

Cook mushrooms and asparagus in ¼ cup dressing in large skillet just until tender, stirring frequently. Add remaining dressing, tomatoes, pasta and chicken; cook, covered, 5 minutes or until heated through. Makes 4 servings.

Chicken Fettuccine

8 ounces fettuccine, uncooked
3 cups chopped assorted vegetables
2 tablespoons olive oil
½ pound boneless skinless chicken breasts, cut into strips
1 cup milk
4 ounces cream cheese, cubed
1 cup shredded Parmesan cheese

Prepare pasta as directed on package, adding vegetables during last 3 minutes of cooking; drain. Heat oil in skillet on medium heat. Add chicken; cook and stir 8 minutes or until cooked through. Remove chicken; set aside. Heat milk, cream cheese and ¾ cup Parmesan cheese in skillet on low heat, stirring constantly until mixture is smooth. Toss all ingredients. Sprinkle with remaining Parmesan cheese. Makes 4 servings.

Crispy Chicken with Honey Dipping Sauce

1 cup salad dressing
¼ cup honey
2 tablespoons Dijon mustard
2 tablespoons peanut butter
Four 1¼-pound boneless, skinless chicken breasts, cut into strips
1½ cups finely crushed potato chips

Mix salad dressing, honey, Dijon mustard and peanut butter. Brush chicken with ½ cup of dressing mixture; coat with crushed chips. Place on greased cookie sheet. Bake at 425 degrees for 7 to 9 minutes or until lightly browned. Serve with remaining dressing mixture as dipping sauce. Makes 8 servings.

Jumpin' Jambalaya

½ cup chopped celery
½ cup chopped onion
1 green pepper, cut into thin strips
1 tablespoon oil
2 boneless skinless chicken breasts, cut into strips
2 tablespoons Creole seasoning, divided
14½-ounce can diced tomatoes
1 cup water
½ pound medium shrimp, peeled and deveined
8-ounce can tomato sauce
2 cups instant rice, uncooked

Cook and stir celery, onion and green pepper in oil in large skillet until tender. Coat chicken with 1 tablespoon of the seasoning. Add to skillet. Cook and stir 2 to 3 minutes or until cooked through. Stir in tomatoes, water, shrimp, tomato sauce and remaining seasoning. Bring to a boil; simmer 2 minutes. Stir in rice; cover. Remove from heat. Let stand 5 minutes. Makes 4 to 6 servings.

Zippy Orange Chicken and Rice

½ cup salad dressing, divided
Four ¼-pound boneless skinless chicken breasts, cut into strips
½ cup orange juice
2 tablespoons brown sugar
1½ cups instant rice, uncooked
1 green pepper, cut into strips
11-ounce can mandarin orange segments, drained
8-ounce can pineapple chunks, drained

Heat 2 tablespoons dressing in skillet on medium-high heat. Add chicken; cook and stir 5 minutes or until no longer pink. Drain. Reduce heat to medium. Mix remaining dressing, orange juice and brown sugar. Stir into skillet. Add rice and green pepper; bring to a boil. Remove from heat; add orange segments and pineapple. Let stand, covered, 5 minutes. Makes 4 servings.

Southern Oven-Fried Chicken

⅓ cup flour
1 teaspoon salt
Dash of pepper
3 to 3½ pound chicken, cut up
1 egg, beaten
2 tablespoons water
½ cup grated Parmesan cheese
½ cup crushed corn flakes
¼ cup butter or margarine, melted

Mix flour and seasonings; coat chicken. Dip chicken in combined egg and water; coat with combined cheese and crushed corn flakes. Place chicken in 9 x 13-inch baking dish; drizzle with butter. Bake at 375 degrees for 1 hour or until chicken is cooked through. Makes 4 servings.

After Holidays Turkey Pot Pie

1 can mixed vegetables, drained
2 cans cream of potato soup
¼ cup milk
Salt and pepper, to taste
2 cups diced, cooked turkey
1 partially cooked pie shell
1 uncooked pie shell

Mix first 5 ingredients and pour into partially cooked pie shell; top with uncooked pie shell. Bake at 350 degrees for 25 minutes. Makes 4 servings.

*Note: Can use canned or homemade biscuits on top instead of pie.

Quick Turkey Divan

20 ounces frozen broccoli, cooked and drained
4 cups cooked, chopped turkey
2 cans cream of chicken soup
1 cup low-fat mayonnaise
½ cup shredded sharp cheese
1 can mushrooms
½ cup bread crumbs
Parmesan cheese
1 cup water chestnuts
1 teaspoon curry powder
½ stick butter, melted
Juice of 1 lemon

Arrange broccoli in a 9x13-inch baking dish. Place turkey on top of broccoli. Combine next 8 ingredients and pour over turkey. Top with melted butter and sprinkle lemon juice over all. Bake at 350 degrees for 1 hour and 15 minutes. Makes 6 to 8 servings.

Crowd Pleasing Enchilada Casserole

1 can diced tomatoes
1½ cans chicken broth
2 tablespoons corn starch, mixed with ½ cup water
8 ounces cream cheese, softened
⅓ cup milk
Chopped onion, to taste
Pressed garlic, to taste
Salt and pepper, to taste
2 large chicken breasts, cooked and cubed
Corn tortillas
Shredded Cheddar and Monterey Jack cheeses

Heat tomatoes and broth, adding cornstarch to thicken. Cook on low until thick like a gravy. Set aside to cool. Mix cream cheese and milk until smooth. Add seasonings and chicken. Set aside. Pour tomato sauce in bottom of 9 x 13-inch baking dish. Layer tortillas and chicken ending with tortillas. Top with cheeses. Bake at 350 degrees for 20 to 25 minutes.

Hoppin' John

Three 15½-ounce cans black-eyed peas, drained and rinsed
Two 13¾-ounce cans chicken broth
16-ounce package turkey smoked sausage, thinly sliced and browned
2 cups chopped onion
1 cup water
1 teaspoon crushed red pepper flakes
½ teaspoon ground red pepper
2½ cups instant long grain rice, uncooked
Chopped parsley

Place black-eyed peas, broth, sausage, onions, water and seasonings in medium saucepan; bring to a boil. Stir in rice; cover. Simmer 10 minutes or until rice is tender. Garnish with chopped parsley. Makes 8 to 10 servings.

Under the Mistletoe Pork Chops and Rice

2 cups instant rice, uncooked
4 pork chops, ¾-inch thick
1 teaspoon Cajun seasoning
2 tablespoons butter or margarine, melted
½ cup chopped onion
2 cups milk
10¾-ounce can cream of mushroom soup

Place rice in bottom of 9 x 13-inch baking dish. Place pork chops over rice in dish. In a separate bowl mix seasoning, butter, onion, milk and soup. Pour over pork chops and rice.   Bake at 350 degrees for 30 minutes.   Makes 4 servings.

Homespun Ham Casserole

2 cups frozen broccoli flowerets, thawed
1½ cups coarsely chopped ham
1½ cups rotini pasta, cooked and drained
½ cup mayonnaise
½ green or red pepper, chopped
¼ cup milk
1½ cups shredded Cheddar cheese, divided
Seasoned croutons

Preheat oven to 350 degrees. Mix all ingredients except ½ cup of cheese and croutons. Pour into 1½-quart casserole dish. Sprinkle with remaining ½ cup cheese. Bake for 30 minutes or until thoroughly heated. Sprinkle with seasoned croutons. Makes 6 servings.

For the microwave: Prepare as directed. Microwave on HIGH 8 to 10 minutes or until thoroughly heated. Sprinkle with seasoned croutons.

Elegant Raspberry-Glazed Pork Chops

1 teaspoon butter or margarine
4 boneless pork chops, about ¾-inch thick
½ cup seedless raspberry jam
⅓ cup raspberry or balsamic vinegar
¼ cup Dijon mustard
1 teaspoon grated orange peel
1½ teaspoons chopped thyme leaves

Heat butter over medium-high heat. Add pork chops; cook on both sides about 5 to 7 minutes or until browned. Stir remaining ingredients together and add to skillet. Simmer, uncovered, until sauce is reduced to a glaze consistency and chops are tender, about 5 minutes, turning chops frequently. Makes 4 servings.

Home for the Holidays Casserole

4 to 6 potatoes, thinly sliced
2 tablespoons oil
1 onion, sliced
1 green pepper, sliced
½ pound diced ham
4 slices Swiss cheese

Fry potatoes in oil. Add onion, green pepper and ham. Stir as needed and season to taste. After potatoes are done place Swiss cheese on top. Turn heat off and allow cheese to melt. Serve from the skillet.

From the Shore Casserole

1 package macaroni shells
¼ cup chopped onion
¼ cup chopped red or green pepper
4 tablespoons butter or margarine, divided
8-ounce package imitation crab meat
1 cup frozen peas, thawed and drained
½ cup mayonnaise
⅓ cup corn flake crumbs
¼ teaspoon onion salt

Prepare macaroni as directed on package; drain. In a small skillet cook and stir onion and pepper in 2 tablespoons of butter until tender. Add to macaroni. Stir in crab meat, peas and mayonnaise. Spoon into 1½-quart casserole dish; cover. Bake at 350 degrees for 15 minutes. Melt remaining butter. Stir in crumbs and onion salt. Uncover casserole; top with crumb mixture. Continue baking, uncovered, 5 to 10 minutes or until golden brown and thoroughly heated. Makes 6 servings.

May substitute 1 can tuna or 1 can salmon for imitation crab meat.

Garlic Shrimp

8 ounces linguine
1 pound medium shrimp, cooked and cleaned
½ pound pea pods
1 cup roasted garlic salad dressing mix

Cook pasta as directed on package, adding shrimp and pea pods during last 2 minutes of cooking time; drain. Toss all ingredients. Serve hot or refrigerate until ready to serve. Makes 4 servings.

Lemon Broccoli Fish

4 sole fillets
2 tablespoons lemon juice
Ground black pepper
10-ounce package frozen broccoli spears, thawed
¼ pound Velveeta, cut up
¼ cup skim milk
½ teaspoon grated lemon peel
½ teaspoon dill weed

Sprinkle each fillet with lemon juice and pepper. Arrange broccoli spears on narrow end of each fish fillet; roll up. Secure with toothpicks. Place, seam side down, in 6 x 10-inch microwavable baking dish; cover. Microwave on HIGH 5 to 7 minutes or until fish flakes easily with fork. In a separate dish microwave remaining ingredients 2 to 3 minutes or until sauce is smooth, stirring after each minute. Remove toothpicks and pour sauce over fillets before serving. Makes 4 servings.

Santa's Spicy Shrimp

12 ounces frozen breaded shrimp
½ cup mayonnaise
2 jalapeño peppers, seeded and minced
2 tablespoons chopped green onion
1 garlic clove, minced
¼ teaspoon ground red pepper
1 loaf French bread, partially split
1 cup finely shredded lettuce
½ cup chopped tomato

Bake shrimp as directed on package. Mix mayonnaise, jalapeño peppers, onion, garlic and red pepper. Spread mixture on bread. Top with shrimp, lettuce and tomato. Cut into 4 pieces. Makes 4 servings.

Seaside Baked Fish Casserole

3 medium potatoes, diced
2 large carrots, sliced
1½ to 2 pounds orange roughy filets
Butter, to taste
Lemon juice, to taste
Garlic powder, to taste
Seasoned salt and pepper, to taste
8-ounce can green peas
8-ounce can corn
14½-ounce can whole tomatoes, drained and cut up
2 to 3 medium onion, sliced
1 teaspoon sugar

Let potatoes and carrots boil for 5 minutes and drain. Place fish on 2 layers of heavy duty foil. Season each piece of fish with seasonings. Pour vegetables in and season. Sprinkle with sugar. Wrap tightly and place on lined cookie sheet. Cook at 375 degrees for 1 hour and 20 minutes.

Desserts

Luscious Lemon Cheesecake

16 ounces cream cheese, softened
½ cup sugar
1 tablespoon lemon juice
½ teaspoon grated lemon peel
½ teaspoon vanilla
2 eggs
One 9-inch graham cracker crumb crust
Whipped topping, thawed
Lemon slices

Mix cream cheese, sugar, lemon juice, lemon peel and vanilla with electric mixer on medium speed until well blended. Add eggs; mix until blended. Pour into crust. Bake at 350 degrees for 40 minutes or until center is almost set. Cool. Refrigerate 3 hours or overnight. Garnish with whipped topping and lemon slices. Makes 8 servings.

Christmas Spice Cake

1 spice cake mix
1 can pumpkin
3 eggs
Whipped topping

Combine all ingredients except whipped topping. Spray microwavable fluted bundt pan with vegetable oil. Place ingredients into pan. Put in microwave for approximately 15 minutes, depending on your microwave. Take out of microwave and cool for 3 minutes. Turn out onto serving plate and let cool completely. Place a dopple of whipped topping onto each piece of cake when serving.

Peppermint Pie

2 cups chocolate wafer cookies, crushed
1½ cups skim milk
¼ teaspoon peppermint extract
1 small package pistachio instant pudding
2 cups whipped topping, thawed
1 square semi-sweet baking chocolate, grated
2 chocolate wafer cookies, quartered

Sprinkle cookie crumbs into 8-inch pie plate which has been sprayed with non stick cooking spray; set aside. Mix milk and extract. Add pudding and beat with wire whisk until well blended. Gently stir in whipped topping and chocolate. Spoon into prepared pie plate. Garnish with quartered wafers. Freeze until firm, about 6 hours. Remove from freezer and let stand about 10 minutes to soften before serving. Store any leftover pie in freezer. Makes 8 servings.

Celebration Apple Pie

8 ounces cream cheese, softened
2 tablespoons sugar
1 tablespoon milk
1 teaspoon vanilla
9-inch baked pastry shell, cooked and cooled
⅔ cup water
½ cup sugar
¼ cup red cinnamon candies
4 cups sliced, peeled apples
1 tablespoon lemon juice
2 teaspoons cornstarch

Mix cream cheese, 2 tablespoons sugar, milk and vanilla until well blended. Spread onto bottom of crust. Heat water, ½ cup sugar and candies on low heat; stir until candy is melted. Add apples; continue cooking 8 to 10 minutes or until apples are tender. Drain, reserving ½ cup liquid.

Mix reserved liquid, lemon juice and cornstarch in saucepan. Stirring constantly, bring to a boil on medium heat. Boil 1 minute. Arrange apples over cream cheese mixture; cover with glaze. Refrigerate. Makes 6 to 8 servings.

The Georgia Peach Pie

4 cups peach slices
¾ cup sugar
¼ cup instant tapioca
1 tablespoon lemon juice
Two 9-inch pie crusts
1 tablespoon margarine

Mix peaches, sugar, tapioca and lemon juice. Let stand 15 minutes. Heat oven to 350 degrees. Roll 1 crust to 11-inch circle on lightly floured surface. Line 9-inch pie plate with pastry, allowing ½-inch overhang. Fill with peach mixture. Dot with margarine. Roll remaining crust to 12-inch circle. Cover pie; seal and flute edge. Cut several slits to permit steam to escape. Bake 30 to 40 minutes or until juices form bubbles that burst slowly. Cool.

For lattice top crust: Roll second crust to 12-inch circle. Cut into ten ½-inch strips with pastry wheel or knife. Place 5 of the strips over filling. Weave lattice crust with remaining strips by folding back alternate strips as each cross strip is added. Fold trimmed edge of lower pastry over ends of strips; seal and flute edge. Bake as directed above.

Triple Berry Pie

1½ cups raspberries
1½ cups strawberries, sliced
1 cup blueberries
9-inch pastry shell, baked and cooled
¾ cup sugar
3 tablespoons cornstarch
1½ cups water
1 small package strawberry gelatin
8 ounces whipped topping

Mix berries in large bowl. Pour into pastry shell. Mix sugar and cornstarch in saucepan. Gradually stir in water until smooth. Stirring constantly, cook on medium heat until mixture comes to a boil; boil 1 minute. Remove from heat. Stir in gelatin until completely dissolved. Cool to room temperature. Pour over berries in pastry shell. Refrigerate 3 hours or until firm. Spread whipped topping over pie before serving. Store leftover pie in refrigerator. Makes 8 servings.

Banana Brownie Pie

1 unbaked pastry shell
1 cup chocolate chips
¼ cup butter
1 small can sweetened condensed milk
¾ cup biscuit mix
2 eggs
1 tablespoon vanilla
2 ripe bananas, sliced

Preheat oven to 375 degrees. Bake pastry shell 10 minutes. Remove from oven and reduce to 325 degrees. Melt chocolate chips and butter over low heat. Beat chocolate mixture with milk, biscuit mix, eggs and vanilla until smooth. Place bananas on bottom of shell and pour chocolate mixture over bananas. Bake 50 to 60 minutes or until set.

Fireside Cranberry Apple Cobbler

5 cups sliced, peeled apples
1¼ cups sugar
1 cup cranberries
3 tablespoons tapioca
½ teaspoon ground cinnamon
1 cup water
2 tablespoons butter or margarine
¾ cup flour
2 tablespoons sugar
1 teaspoon baking powder
⅛ teaspoon salt
¼ cup butter or margarine
3 tablespoons milk

Mix apples, 1¼ cups sugar, cranberries, tapioca, cinnamon and water in large saucepan. Let stand 5 minutes. Stirring constantly, cook on medium heat until mixture comes to a full boil. Pour into 2-quart baking dish. Dot with 2 tablespoons butter. Mix flour, 2 tablespoons sugar, baking powder and salt. Cut in ¼ cup butter until mixture resembles coarse crumbs. Stir in milk until soft dough forms. Drop dough by tablespoonfuls onto hot apple mixture. Bake at 375 degrees for 30 minutes or until topping is golden brown. Serve warm with whipped topping or ice cream. Makes 8 servings.

Heavenly Peach Strudel

1¼ cups all-purpose flour
½ cup sour cream
½ cup butter or margarine, softened
12-ounce jar peach preserves
½ cup flaked coconut
¼ cup finely chopped pecans
Powdered sugar

Beat first 3 ingredients at medium speed until blended. Shape into a ball; cover with plastic wrap. Chill at least 1 hour. Divide dough in half. Roll each portion into a 13 x 6-inch rectangle on a well-floured surface. Spread preserves evenly over rectangles, leaving a ½-inch border. Sprinkle with coconut and pecans. Roll up, jelly roll fashion, starting at long side; pinch seams and ends to seal. Place rolls, seam side down, 3 inches apart on a large baking sheet. Bake at 450 degrees for 18 minutes. Let cool. Sprinkle with powdered sugar; cut diagonally into slices. Makes 20 servings.

Cream Cheese Flan

12-ounce can evaporated milk
8-ounce package cream cheese, cubed
2 cups sugar, divided
5 eggs
1 teaspoon vanilla
Dash of salt

Place milk and cream cheese in blender; cover. Blend until smooth. Add 1 cup of sugar, eggs, vanilla and salt. Blend until smooth. Pour mixture into 9-inch mold caramelized with 1 cup sugar. Cover with foil. Bake in water bath at 350 degrees for 1½ hours. Refrigerate overnight before unmolding. Makes 8 servings.

For coconut variation: Omit vanilla. Add ¼ cup coconut or ½ cup coconut milk and 1 tablespoon rum.

Raspberry White Chocolate Mousse

10-ounce package sweetened frozen raspberries, thawed
2 tablespoons sugar
1 tablespoon orange juice concentrate
2 cups whipping cream
6 ounces white baking chocolate
1 teaspoon vanilla
¼ cup chocolate chips
1 teaspoon vegetable oil

In a blender combine raspberries, sugar and orange juice concentrate; cover and process until smooth. Press through a sieve; discard seeds. Refrigerate sauce. Cook and stir whipping cream and white chocolate over low heat until chocolate is melted. Stir in vanilla. Transfer to a mixing bowl. Cover and refrigerate for 6 hours or until thickened, stirring occasionally. Beat cream mixture on high speed until light and fluffy, about 1 to 2 minutes. Before serving melt chocolate chips and oil in microwave or saucepan. Spoon 2 tablespoons of raspberry sauce on each plate. Pipe or spoon 2 cups chocolate mouse over sauce; drizzle with melted chocolate. Store leftovers in the refrigerator. Makes 8 servings.

Red and Green Holiday Mold

2½ cups boiling water
1 large package gelatin, any red flavor
1 cup cold water
1 small package lime gelatin
1 cup vanilla ice cream, softened

Stir 1½ cups boiling water into red gelatin. Stir 2 minutes or until completely dissolved. Stir in cold water. Reserve 1½ cups gelatin at room temperature. Pour remaining red gelatin into wreath or 5 cup mold which has been sprayed with non stick cooking spray. Refrigerate about 45 minutes or until set.

Stir remaining boiling water into lime gelatin. Stir 2 minutes or until completely dissolved. Spoon in ice cream, stirring until melted and smooth. Spoon over red layer in mold. Refrigerate about 20 minutes or until set.

Spoon reserved red gelatin over creamy layer in mold. Refrigerate 4 hours or until firm. Unmold. Garnish as desired. Store leftover gelatin mold in refrigerator. Makes 10 servings.

Dirt Cups for the Little Elves

16-ounce package chocolate sandwich cookies
2 cups cold milk
1 small package chocolate instant pudding
8-ounce package whipped topping, thawed
Eight 8-ounce paper or plastic cups
Gummy worms

Crush cookies in plastic bag with rolling pin or in food processor. Mix cold milk and pudding. Beat with wire whisk 2 minutes. Let stand 5 minutes. Stir in whipped topping and ½ of crushed cookies. Place about 1 tablespoon crushed cookies into each cup. Fill cups about ¾ full with pudding mixture. Top with remaining crushed cookies. Refrigerate until ready to serve. Garnish with gummy worms just before serving. Makes 8 servings.

Rocky Road Brownies

20-ounce package sugar cookie dough
16-ounce container caramel apple dip
2 tablespoons water
1 cup chocolate chips
1 cup chopped peanuts
2 cups miniature marshmallows

Press cookie dough onto bottom and one inch up sides of 9 x 13-inch baking dish. Bake at 350 degrees for 15 to 18 minutes or until lightly browned. Pour caramel mixture over crust; top with chocolate chips, peanuts and marshmallows. Broil 5 inches from heat for 1 minute or until marshmallows are lightly browned. Cool; cut into bars. Makes 2 dozen.

May substitute refrigerated peanut butter cookies for sugar cookies.

Candies & Cookies

Snow Balls

1 cup peanut butter chips
¾ cup butter
½ cup cocoa
14-ounce can sweetened condensed milk
1 tablespoon vanilla
Powdered sugar

Melt chips and butter on low heat. Stir in cocoa until smooth. Add milk and vanilla. Cook and stir until thick and well blended. Remove from heat and chill at least 2 hours or until firm. Shape into 1-inch balls and roll in powdered sugar. Refrigerate until ready to serve.

Marilyn's Christmas Candy

1 pound powdered sugar
1 cup coconut
1 cup chopped pecans
1 teaspoon vanilla
1 cup graham cracker crumbs
½ cup crunchy peanut butter
1 cup butter, melted
½ bar paraffin
6 ounces semi-sweet chocolate chips

Thoroughly mix sugar, coconut, pecans, vanilla and graham cracker crumbs into the peanut butter. Pour melted butter over mixture and blend well. Shape dough into balls. Melt paraffin and chocolate chips together over boiling water. Using a toothpick dip balls into the chocolate and place on waxed paper.

Caramel Candy made Simple

2 sticks butter
1 pound light brown sugar
1 cup white corn syrup
1 can sweetened condensed milk
1 teaspoon vanilla

Melt butter in a 3-quart bowl in the microwave for 1 minute. Add brown sugar, syrup and milk. Mix well. Microwave on HIGH for 15½ minutes, stirring every 5 minutes. Add vanilla; pour into a buttered 9 x 13-inch casserole dish. Let stand for 2 hours before cutting.

Georgian Pecan Fudge

4 cups sugar
½ pound butter
½ pound pecan pieces
1 cup white corn syrup
1 cup plus 2 tablespoons evaporated milk
½ teaspoon salt
1 teaspoon vanilla

Boil all ingredients except vanilla to 240 degrees or soft ball stage. Cool 25 minutes. Add vanilla and beat until thick. Pour into buttered pan.

Holiday Pecan Balls

1 cup flour
¼ pound margarine, melted
1 tablespoon sugar
1 cup chopped pecans
1 teaspoon vanilla
Powdered Sugar

Mix ingredients together by hand, then roll into small balls. Bake for 30 minutes at 350 degrees. Cool. Roll in powered sugar.

Easy Christmas Candy

1 bag peanut butter chips
1 bag semi-sweet chocolate chips
1 bag butterscotch chips
1 bag milk chocolate chips
1 can mixed nuts
Raisins

Mix all chips together; microwave until melted. Add nuts and raisins. Spoon into baking cups. Allow to set and put into gift boxes.

Yuletide Candy Bars

1 jar creamy peanut butter
1 bag milk chocolate chips
1 bag mini marshmallows

Mix peanut butter and chocolate chips over medium heat. When melted add marshmallows, a hand full or two at a time, letting them melt before adding more. Stir constantly so that it does not stick. Place the mixture on a cookie sheet covered with wax paper or foil, flatten out to all edges. Run a knife through the mix to cut the size of bars you would like. Cover and put into the refrigerator or freezer; when solid start eating.

Snow Candy

1 pound white chocolate bark candy
1 pound salted pecans
2 cups crispy rice cereal

Melt candy in a double boiler. Add pecans and cereal. Mix well. Spoon onto waxed paper. Refrigerate until firm. Break into pieces; store in airtight container.

Everyone's Favorite Peanut Brittle

2 cups sugar
1 cup light corn syrup
1 cup water
2 cups unroasted peanuts
¼ teaspoon salt
1 teaspoon butter
1 teaspoon soda
1 teaspoon vanilla

Combine sugar, corn syrup and water. Cook to 236 degrees. Add peanuts and salt; cook to 295 degrees or hard crack stage. Remove and immediately add butter, soda and vanilla. It will foam so stir constantly; pour quickly into a 9 x 13-inch buttered pan. Allow to harden.

Holiday Sugar Cookies

8 ounces cream cheese, softened
1 cup butter or margarine
⅔ cup sugar
¼ teaspoon vanilla
2 cups flour
Colored sugar

Beat cream cheese, butter, sugar and vanilla with electric mixer on medium speed until well blended. Add flour; mix well. Refrigerate several hours or overnight.

Roll dough to ¼-inch thickness on lightly floured surface. Cut into shapes; sprinkle with colored sugar. Place on ungreased cookie sheet. Bake at 350 degrees for 12 to 15 minutes or until edges are lightly browned. Makes 3½ dozen.

Oatmeal Scotchies

1 cup all-purpose flour
1 teaspoon baking soda
½ teaspoon salt
½ teaspoon cinnamon
1 cup butter, softened
¾ cup sugar
¾ cup packed brown sugar
2 eggs
1 teaspoon vanilla
3 cups uncooked oats
12-ounce package butterscotch chips

Preheat oven to 375 degrees. Combine flour, soda, salt and cinnamon; set aside. Combine butter, sugar, brown sugar, eggs and vanilla; beat until creamy. Gradually add flour mixture. Stir in oats and butterscotch chips. Spread dough into greased 15½ x 10½ x1-inch baking sheet. Bake for 20 to 25 minutes. Cool completely and cut into squares.

Can be made into cookies by dropping by spoonfuls onto ungreased cookie sheet and baking for 7 to 8 minutes.

Molasses Spice Crisps

2½ cups flour
2 teaspoons baking soda
2 teaspoons cloves
2 teaspoons ginger
2 teaspoons cinnamon
¾ cup shortening
1 cup sugar
1 egg
4 tablespoons molasses
Sugar, for dipping

Mix together flour, baking soda and spices. Cream shortening and sugar; mixing well. Add egg, beat well, then add molasses. Add flour mixture gradually. Chill dough. Roll in balls the size of walnuts, dip in sugar. Place sugar side up on a greased cookie sheet. Bake at 350 degrees for 15 to 20 minutes. Makes at least 4 dozen.

Strawberry Pretzel Squares

2 cups finely crushed pretzels
⅓ cup sugar
⅔ cup butter or margarine, melted
12 ounces cream cheese, softened
¼ cup sugar
2 tablespoons milk
1 cup whipped topping, thawed
2 cups boiling water
1 large package strawberry gelatin
1½ cups cold water
2 pints strawberries, sliced

Mix crushed pretzels, ⅓ cup sugar and butter; press firmly into bottom of 9 x 13-inch baking dish. Bake at 350 degrees for 10 minutes. Cool. Beat cream cheese, ¼ cup sugar and milk until smooth. Gently stir in whipped topping. Spread over crust. Refrigerate.

Meanwhile, stir boiling water into gelatin at least 2 minutes or until completely dissolved. Stir in cold water. Refrigerate 1½ hours or until thickened. Stir in strawberries. Spoon over cheese layer. Refrigerate 3 hours or until firm. Cut into squares. Garnish with additional whipped topping. Makes 15 to 18 servings.

Cinnamon Cookies

3½ cups flour
1 teaspoon baking soda
1 teaspoon cinnamon
¼ teaspoon salt
1 cup shortening or margarine
1 cup brown sugar
1 cup sugar
2 eggs
1 cup chopped nuts

Sift flour, baking soda, cinnamon and salt together. Cream shortening; adding brown sugar and sugar gradually. Beat eggs and stir into creamed mixture. Stir in dry ingredients 1 cupful at a time. Add nuts. Divide dough in half and place each half on sheet of waxed paper. Roll into long thin rolls; wrap in waxed paper and store in refrigerator for 12 hours or overnight.

To bake, pull off paper and slice cookies. Bake on well greased cookie sheet at 350 degrees for 7 to 10 minutes. Makes about 8 dozen.

Gift Giving Goodies

The Best Chocolate Brickle

Vegetable cooking spray
12 graham crackers
1 cup butter or margarine
1 cup sugar
12 ounces semi-sweet chocolate morsels
6 ounces almond brickle chips

Line a 15x10x1-inch pan with foil and coat with spray. Place graham crackers in a single layer in prepared pan and set aside. Combine butter and sugar in saucepan. Bring to a boil over medium heat, stirring constantly. Boil 1½ to 2 minutes, without stirring. Pour mixture over graham crackers. Bake at 350 degrees for 5 minutes. Remove from the oven and sprinkle with chocolate chips. Let stand until morsels are soft enough to spread. Spread smoothly over top. Sprinkle with brickle, press lightly. Cool and cut into 1½-inch squares. Makes 5 dozen squares.

Gift Pecan Squares

2 cups all-purpose flour
½ cup powdered sugar
1 cup butter or margarine
14-ounce can sweetened condensed milk
1 large egg
1 teaspoon vanilla
7.5-ounce package almond brickle chips
1 cup chopped pecans

Combine flour and powdered sugar. Cut in butter with a pastry blender until crumbly. Press mixture evenly into a greased 9 x 13-inch pan. Bake at 350 degrees for 15 minutes. Stir together condensed milk and remaining ingredients until well blended; pour over crust. Bake at 350 degrees for 25 minutes or until golden. Cool and cut into squares. Makes 4 dozen.

Pecan Biscotti for your Hostess

Cooking spray
2 cups flour
1½ teaspoons baking powder
¼ teaspoon baking soda
⅛ teaspoon salt
¼ cup margarine or butter
⅔ cup packed brown sugar
2 eggs
⅓ cup finely chopped pecans

Spray a large cookie sheet with cooking spray. Set aside. Stir together flour, baking powder, baking soda and salt. Set aside. Beat butter for 30 seconds. Add brown sugar and beat until well combined. Add eggs; beat well. Stir in flour mixture and pecans. On waxed paper shape dough into two 12-inch logs. Place on prepared baking sheet. Flatten logs slightly. Bake at 375 degrees for 15 to 18 minutes or until lightly brown. Cool completely on wire racks about 1 hour. Cut each log diagonally into ½-inch thick slices. Arrange slices, cut side down on the baking sheet. Bake at 325 degrees for 5 minutes. Turn slices over; bake about 5 minutes longer until crisp and dry. Cool completely on wire racks. Makes 38 to 40.

Sugar and Spice and Everything Nice Pecans

¾ cup sugar
1 egg white
2½ tablespoons water
1 teaspoon ground cinnamon
½ teaspoon salt
¼ teaspoon allspice
¼ teaspoon ground cloves
¼ teaspoon ground nutmeg
8 cups pecan halves

Combine first 8 ingredients and mix well. Add pecans and stir until evenly coated. Spread pecans in a greased jelly roll pan. Bake at 275 degrees for 50 to 55 minutes. Remove to waxed paper and let cool. Makes 9 cups.

Aioli

4 large cloves garlic, minced
¼ cup egg product
2 tablespoons lemon juice
¼ teaspoon salt
¼ cup olive oil

Combine garlic, egg product, lemon juice and salt. Blend until thoroughly combined. Gradually add oil in a thin, steady stream. Place in a covered container and refrigerate until ready to serve. This is perfect as a dip or as a substitution for mayonnaise. Makes about 1 cup.

Spicy Horseradish Dip

1 cup mayonnaise
2 tablespoons prepared horseradish
1 teaspoon cider or white vinegar
½ teaspoon curry powder
½ teaspoon garlic salt
½ teaspoon ground mustard

Combine all ingredients. Cover and chill for at least one hour. Makes 1 cup.

Housewarming Horseradish Mustard

1 tablespoon cornstarch
¼ teaspoon salt
2 teaspoons dry mustard
¼ cup cider vinegar
2 teaspoons prepared horseradish
¾ cup hot water
2 teaspoons honey
1 egg yolk

Combine first 3 ingredients in saucepan; stir in vinegar and horseradish. Slowly stir in hot water and honey. Cook over low heat, stirring constantly, until thickened and bubbly. Beat egg yolk; gradually add ¼ mixture to egg yolk. Pour egg yolk mixture into saucepan; stir constantly for 1 minute. Cover and chill 3 hours. Makes ¾ cup.

Wish List Peach Chutney

1½ pounds peaches
1 cup golden raisins
1 cup packed light brown sugar
¾ cup cider vinegar
½ cup coarsely chopped walnuts
1 cinnamon stick
½ teaspoon ground ginger
½ teaspoon salt
½ teaspoon ground red pepper

Combine all ingredients, stirring until sugar is dissolved. Cook over medium heat, stirring occasionally, until thickened. Serve with grilled chicken.

Spicy Holiday Sauce

10-ounce jar pineapple preserves or topping
10-ounce jar apple jelly
¼ cup dry mustard
⅓ cup prepared horseradish
1½ teaspoons pepper

Combine all ingredients and blend in blender or food processor. Makes 2½ cups and may be stored in airtight container in refrigerator. When ready to serve, spoon over cream cheese and serve with crackers.

Warm Mocha Mix

½ cup instant espresso granules or coffee granules
¼ cup unsweetened cocoa
¼ cup non-dairy creamer
6 tablespoons powdered sugar

Combine all ingredients; mix well. To serve, spoon 1 to 2 tablespoons mix into cup. Add ¾ cup boiling water; stir to dissolve. Garnish with whipped cream and a pinch of cocoa. Serve immediately.

Super Duper Ice Cream Topping

1 cup chocolate syrup
1 cup chocolate chips
½ cup caramel
1 ground Twix candy bar

Mix all ingredients well. May be stored in jar. Do not refrigerate.

Special Holiday Potpourri

4 oranges
4 lemons
½ cup whole cloves
½ cup whole allspice
10 cinnamon sticks, broken
10 bay leaves, crumbled

Peel oranges and lemons, being careful to remove only peel. Cut peel into 1-inch pieces. Spread peel on a towel-lined pan. Bake at 175 degrees for 1 to 1½ hours, tossing occasionally. Peels should be slightly crunchy. When finished baking, spread peels and let air dry for 24 hours. Combine dry peels with remaining ingredients. Makes 3 to 4 half-pints.

To use, put 1 tablespoon of mixture into jar. Add water and microwave on HIGH for 2 minutes to heat water and release fragrance. Reheat as needed.

Zucchini Marmalade for your Hostess

6 cups peeled and shredded zucchini
½ cup lemon juice
1 cup crushed pineapple, drained
1 package Sure Jell
6 cups sugar
6 ounces favorite flavor gelatin

Cook zucchini for 1 hour on low heat. Add lemon juice, pineapple and Sure Jell; stir well. Add sugar and cook 6 minutes, then stir in gelatin while hot. Pour into 4 one-pint jars and seal.

Derby Afternoon Cheese Straws

½ pound grated extra sharp Cheddar cheese
¼ pound softened butter
½ teaspoon salt
⅛ teaspoon cayenne pepper
1½ cups flour

Combine all ingredients into a dough that is soft and pliable. You may want to add a few drops of water. Roll out dough on a lightly floured board. Cut into strips with a sharp knife or pizza cutter. Place on a shiny ungreased baking sheet. Bake at 325 degrees for 20 minutes until straws begin to brown very lightly around the edges. Let cool on baking sheet. If desired, sprinkle lightly with paprika and salt. Store in airtight container between sheets of waxed paper. Makes 6 dozen straws.

Index

Soups and Salads

Other cookbooks by McClanahan Publishing House, Inc.:

A Little Touch of Grace
Cornmeal Country
Curtis Grace: Encore
Delicious & Deliteful
Derby Entertaining
Especially Herbs
Kentucky Keepsakes
Merry Christmas from Kentucky
Merry Christmas from Texas
Merry Christmas from the South
Simply Tennessee
Soccer Mom Cookbook